Isaiah 40–55

Build a Highway for God

A Guided Discovery for Groups and Individuals

Kevin Perrotta

LOYOLA PRESS.
A JESUIT MINISTRY
Chicago

LOYOLAPRESS.
A JESUIT MINISTRY

3441 N. Ashland Avenue
Chicago, Illinois 60657
(800) 621-1008
www.loyolapress.com

Nihil Obstat
Reverend Michael Mulhall, O.Carm.
Censor Deputatus
January 31, 2002

Imprimatur
Most Reverend Raymond E. Goedert, M.A., S.T.L., J.C.L.
Vicar General
Archdiocese of Chicago
February 14, 2002

The Nihil Obstat and *Imprimatur* are official declarations that a book is free of doctrinal and moral error. No implication is contained therein that those who have granted the *Nihil Obstat* and *Imprimatur* agree with the content, opinions, or statements expressed. Nor do they assume any legal responsibility associated with publication.

Dean Hedglen's story (p. 21) first appeared in *Prison Report,* a newsletter of Partners in Evangelism, 9639 Dr. Perry Road, Suite 126, Ijamsville, MD 21754.

The Franciscan Brothers of Peace (p. 53) may be contacted at 1289 Lafond Ave., St. Paul, MN 55104-2035; (651) 646-8586.

The Greek text with English translation of 1 Clement (p. 67) can be found in Kirsopp Lake, trans., ed., *The Apostolic Fathers,* vol. 1, Loeb Classical Library, no. 24 (Cambridge: Harvard University Press, 1985). An older translation may be found at www.ccel.org/fathers2 (click on Volume 1 under Ante-Nicene Fathers). The translation in this book is by Kevin Perrotta.

The Little Sisters of the Poor (p. 77) may be contacted at (410) 744-9367 or through their Web site, www.cmswr.org/MemberCommunities/lsp.htm.

Interior design by Kay Hartmann/Communique Design
Illustration by Charise Mericle Harper

ISBN-13: 978-0-8294-1812-5
ISBN-10: 0-8294-1812-1

Printed in the United States of America
18 19 20 21 22 23 24 25 26 Bang 14 13 12 11 10 9 8 7 6

Contents

How to Use This Guide

You might compare the Bible to a national park. The park is so large that you could spend months, even years, getting to know it. But a brief visit, if carefully planned, can be enjoyable and worthwhile. In a few hours you can drive through the park and pull over at a handful of sites. At each stop you can get out of the car, take a short trail through the woods, listen to the wind blowing through the trees, get a feel for the place.

In this booklet we'll drive through a small portion of the Bible, making half a dozen stops along the way. At those points we'll proceed on foot, taking a leisurely walk through the selected passages. The readings have been chosen to take us to the heart of the message contained in Isaiah 40–55. After each discussion we'll get back in the car and take the highway to the next stop.

This guide provides everything you need to begin exploring this section of Isaiah in six discussions—or to do a six-part exploration on your own. The introduction on page 6 will prepare you to get the most out of your reading. The weekly sections feature key passages in Isaiah 40–55, with explanations that highlight the message of these prophecies for us today. Equally important, each section supplies questions that will launch you into fruitful discussion, helping you to both investigate the passages for yourself and learn from one another. If you're using the booklet by yourself, the questions will spur your personal reflection.

Each discussion is meant to be a *guided discovery.*

Guided. None of us is equipped to read the Bible without help. We read the Bible *for* ourselves but not *by* ourselves. Scripture was written to be understood and applied in the community of faith. So each week "A Guide to the Reading," drawing on the work of both modern biblical scholars and Christian writers of the past, supplies background and explanations. The guide will help you grasp the message of the Isaiah readings. Think of it as a friendly park ranger who points out noteworthy details and explains what you're looking at so you can appreciate things for yourself.

Discovery. The purpose is for *you* to interact with Isaiah. "Questions for Careful Reading" is a tool to help you dig into the text and examine it carefully. "Questions for Application" will help you consider what these words mean for your life here and now. Each week concludes with an "Approach to Prayer" section that helps you respond to God's word. Supplementary "Living Tradition" and "Saints in the Making" sections offer the thoughts and experiences of Christians past and present. By showing what the message of Isaiah has meant to others, these sections will help you consider what Isaiah's words mean for you.

How long are the discussion sessions? We've assumed you will have about an hour and a half when you get together. If you have less time, you'll find that most of the elements can be shortened somewhat.

Is homework necessary? You will get the most out of your discussions if you read the weekly material and prepare your answers to the questions in advance of each meeting. But if participants are not able to prepare, have someone read the "Guide to the Reading" sections aloud at the points where they appear.

What about leadership? If you happen to have a world-class biblical scholar in your group, by all means ask him or her to lead the discussions. But in the absence of any professional Scripture scholars, or even accomplished amateur biblical scholars, you can still have a first-class Bible discussion. Choose two or three people to take turns as facilitators and have everyone read "Suggestions for Bible Discussion Groups" (page 82) before beginning.

Does everyone need a guide? a Bible? Everyone in the group will need his or her own copy of this booklet. It contains the sections of Isaiah that are discussed, so a Bible is not absolutely necessary—but each participant will find it useful to have one. You should have at least one Bible on hand for your discussions. (See page 86 for recommendations.)

How do we get started? Before you begin, take a look at the suggestions for Bible discussion groups (page 82) or individuals (page 85).

Startling Announcements

What discourages you? I can tell you what discourages me. My list runs from the latest news report of ethnic cleansing to the near impossibility of getting a carpenter to come out to my house and make repairs. In the middle of my list of discouragements is the word *me,* with a circle drawn around it. Probably each of us has a list containing our particular sorrows and peeves. Some of us keep the list hidden in a drawer. Others brood over it frequently.

For all of us in our discouragement, God has a message of hope. The message has been delivered by Jesus of Nazareth. In fact, Jesus himself is the heart of the message. If we wish to learn about Jesus and his message, we may go to the Gospels, which provide accounts of his life, his teaching, his death and resurrection. But in order to grasp the meaning of Jesus, it is also helpful to view him in his place in the history of God's dealings with the people of Israel. Jesus was a first-century Palestinian Jew. And he presented himself as the fulfillment of God's interactions with Israel.

God's actions over the centuries led the Jews to certain expectations concerning how God would act in the world in the future. The book from which we are going to read, Isaiah, played a large part in developing these expectations. In the first century, many Jews read the book of Isaiah as a prophecy of what God would soon do. The substantial number of fragments and even entire copies of Isaiah found among the Dead Sea Scrolls testifies to the fascination the book held for the Jewish sect that maintained the library at Qumran. Jesus himself certainly pondered Isaiah and used parts of it to explain himself to his listeners (Luke 4:17–21). After Jesus' death and resurrection, the Church found the book of Isaiah so useful for enriching its picture of Jesus that the book came to be called the fifth Gospel.

The portion of Isaiah that we are going to read—chapters 40 through 55—is especially rich in insights into the significance of Jesus. These chapters of Isaiah are particularly helpful for grasping how Jesus speaks to us in our discouragement, perhaps because they were originally addressed to people in very discouraging circumstances.

While the situation of the original audience is of less concern to us than our own situation, it is useful for us to give it some attention. The message that God spoke through Isaiah—the message that helps us better understand Jesus—comes to us as a series of prophecies directed to Israelites more than twenty-five centuries ago. To grasp what Isaiah's words mean for us today, we need some understanding of what they meant to his original audience. To aid your understanding, this introduction and the "Guide to the Reading" sections offer a little background.

The dominating event behind chapters 40 through 55 of Isaiah is the Babylonians' destruction of Jerusalem in 587 B.C. In the centuries before this catastrophe, the people of the small kingdom of Judah* had strayed from the principles of justice and integrity to which God had called them when he made a covenant with them through Moses. Their straying from God's will was not a matter of a few minor iniquities. The prophets give us a vivid picture of the gross injustices in Judah in the period before the fall of Jerusalem (Jeremiah 5:26–29; 22:3–5, 13–17; 34:8–22; Zephaniah 3.) Injustice and corruption led to dysfunctional political and diplomatic policies. Finally, ignoring sensible prophetic advice (Jeremiah 27), the people of Judah rebelled against the Babylonian empire—and suffered a crushing defeat. The Babylonians destroyed Jerusalem, the capital of Judah, and sent the Judean upper class into exile in Babylon, hundreds of miles to the east (in modern-day Iraq; see 2 Chronicles 36:15–21).

At that point, it looked to some Israelites as though their relationship with God and their existence as a people had simply come to an end. God seemed to have abandoned them. In a vision, the prophet Ezekiel saw God's splendid, awesome, life-giving

*Judah was roughly the hilly area between the Dead Sea and the Mediterranean Sea (it lies in present-day Israeli and Palestinian territories). The residents of the region of Judah were called "Judeans," from which the name *Jews* developed. The term *Jews* became common after the fall of Jerusalem in 587 B.C. Before that, the community of the Mosaic covenant was usually called "the people of Israel" or simply "Israel." After the exile, the geographical term *Judah* tended to be replaced by *Judea.*

presence—his "glory"—departing from Jerusalem (Ezekiel 11:22–23). (Ezekiel was in exile in Babylon at the time he gave his prophecy, which makes his words about God's departure from Jerusalem especially poignant.) There seemed to be no hope for restoration, given the massive reality of the Babylonian empire. In the face of that power, it seemed impossible that the small group of exiles, or the impoverished villagers who remained behind in Judah, could ever rebuild their national life.

Four decades passed. Adults who had been sent into exile became old and died in Babylon. Children grew up with little, if any, recollection of Jerusalem. What happened to the exiles' relationship with God and with one another?

Paradoxically, the shock of defeat had a constructive effect on some of those who were sent off into exile. Many of them had been convinced that God would simply never let them be defeated. They thought of him as a kind of tribal deity who could be relied on to provide protection and blessing for his tribe, regardless of how they behaved. Prophets like Jeremiah had tried unsuccessfully to penetrate this mind-set. They reminded the people of the responsibility to act justly and mercifully that was laid on them by their covenant relationship with God. Then, the breaching of Jerusalem's walls by the Babylonian army tore a breach in the Israelites' complacent picture of a convenient, undemanding God. They now saw with terrible clarity how deeply God cares about justice. He had shown that he was willing to use painful corrective measures to make them pay attention to the priority he places on treating others with integrity and mercy. This shattering realization opened these exiles to a broader, deeper understanding of God. And this, in the midst of their hopeless situation, gave them hope: "Surely this great and just and merciful God has not utterly abandoned us!" Searching for a way forward, the exiles reexamined their national past. They discovered that it was not God who had broken the covenant with them; rather, they had broken the covenant with him. This was the root of the disasters that had befallen them. As they reflected on their history, the exiles identified ways in which Israel had gone astray from God, and they resolved to change. On the basis of their repentant self-examination, they wrote and edited books about Israel's past—books that now form much of the Old Testament.

But defeat and exile did not lead all the exiles to a deeper faith in God. To some Israelites, their situation seemed to demonstrate that God no longer cared about them. To some, it appeared that the God of Israel had proved to be weaker than the gods of Babylon, since the Babylonian army had devastated their little nation. Some Israelites, it seems, slipped into resignation or despair.

Then, suddenly, some forty years after the destruction of Jerusalem, God began to convey a series of startling announcements to the people of Israel. Through a prophet, God announced that he was about to unfold a rescue plan on their behalf. Many of the recipients of this message found it difficult to believe and respond to, because God spoke about accomplishing his purposes in uncomfortable, even unwelcome ways and, perhaps even more, because his promises were almost incredibly wonderful.

Who was the prophet who delivered these messages? His prophecies now constitute chapters 40 through 55 of the book of Isaiah. But most scholars believe he was not the same person as the Isaiah who wrote the earlier chapters. The main reason for this view is that the Isaiah who was responsible for chapters 1 through 29 of the book lived a century before the fall of Jerusalem. The prophet of chapters 40 through 55 lived almost half a century after the city's fall.

We have virtually no information about the prophet of Isaiah 40–55. All we know of this later prophet is what can be inferred from his prophecies—which is not very much. We do not even know his name. Apparently some people in Israel felt that this later prophet's message followed in the tradition of the earlier prophet Isaiah, so they placed the writings of the later prophet in the same scroll with those of the former one. This was in keeping with an ancient practice of associating later writings with notable earlier figures—a phenomenon we find elsewhere in the Bible. Thus the first five books of the Old Testament were ascribed to Moses, the Psalms were connected with David, and some of the wisdom books were linked with Solomon (Proverbs, Ecclesiastes, Wisdom of Solomon). Scholars refer to the prophet of Isaiah 40–55 as

Second Isaiah or (meaning the same thing but using a Greek word) Deutero-Isaiah. Except where it might cause confusion, in this booklet we will refer to him simply as Isaiah.

Needless to say, the fact that the author of Isaiah 40–55 is unknown to us does not in any way lessen the inspired quality of his words. The community of Judaism and, later, the Church have recognized these prophecies as God's word. In fact, large portions of the Bible are of uncertain authorship (the authors of all the historical books from Judges through Maccabees, for example, are anonymous), but this does not detract at all from their truth and authority.

Reading Isaiah's prophecies, you may well wonder what response the Israelites made to God's promises and whether events unfolded according to Isaiah's visions. In order to keep this introduction as short as possible, I have dealt with these questions briefly in an essay at the end of this booklet entitled "What Happened after That?" It surveys developments from Isaiah to Jesus and suggests how Isaiah's prophecies are fulfilled in Jesus—and how they speak to us today. But the main historical developments are these: As Isaiah predicted, a Persian ruler named Cyrus soon conquered the Babylonian empire. He then instituted policies that encouraged the various peoples of his empire to strengthen and renew their ancestral traditions. As part of this policy, Cyrus allowed the Jewish exiles to begin to return to Judea. He even authorized a subsidy for the rebuilding of the temple in Jerusalem (2 Chronicles 36:22–23; Ezra 1–3).

Before closing, I would like to offer a suggestion or two concerning how to go about reading these chapters of Isaiah. You will notice that Isaiah has conveyed his message in poetic form. If we are to benefit from his words, we must keep their form in mind. We should remember that poetry is not designed chiefly to communicate information. Francis Scott Key did not pen "The Star-Spangled Banner" to provide an account of the defense of Fort McHenry. He wrote it to share his exultation in the fortitude of the American forces. We should not expect Isaiah to provide detailed answers to historical or theological questions. Rather we should try to hear the music of Isaiah's prophecies. Isaiah has conveyed his messages in poetry, and poetry speaks to the heart. So let Isaiah move you. As you read, use your imagination to try to recreate the situation of Isaiah's first audience. Feel their discouragement. Then experience their astonishment at God's unexpected announcements through Isaiah. Sense how difficult it was for them to welcome and believe and cooperate with the divine intervention about which Isaiah spoke.

A note about Hebrew poetry may be helpful. It does not use rhyme. Scholars are not even certain whether it uses rhythm or meter—and in any case, there is no rhythm or meter in the English translations. Hebrew poetry, however, has a form that carries over quite well in translation: it is generally structured in somewhat parallel statements. Sometimes the parallel parts express a single thought in two ways ("He gives power to the faint, / and strengthens the powerless"—40:29). Sometimes the second part adds something to the first ("He was cut off from the land of the living, / stricken for the transgression of my people"—53:8). Occasionally the parts express a sharp contrast ("The grass withers, the flower fades; / but the word of our God will stand forever"—40:8). Like poetry in English, Hebrew poetry tends to be dense and filled with imagery.

You will notice various voices in these chapters from Isaiah: the members of God's heavenly court speak to one another, God speaks, the prophet speaks, and even the people speak briefly. One scholar, Klaus Baltzer, has suggested that chapters 40 through 55 of Isaiah were written to be performed as a sort of religious drama somewhere in desolate Jerusalem. Perhaps it was originally "staged" in the courtyard of the shattered temple or on a hillside where the city wall lay in ruins and the ground was covered with the rubble of burned-out buildings. Whether other scholars accept Baltzer's proposal or not, the fallen city of Jerusalem is an evocative setting in which to imagine the prophecies being read. And Baltzer's suggestion is a useful encouragement to read Isaiah's prophecies *aloud.* Isaiah's dramatic poetry may best come alive by being divided into parts and read by several voices (see the suggestions each week in "Opening the Bible").

Finally, if you have a recording of George Frideric Handel's *Messiah,* dig it out. Handel created soaring musical settings for portions of Isaiah that we will read in weeks 1 and 5.

Week 1

Comfort My Discouraged People

Questions to Begin

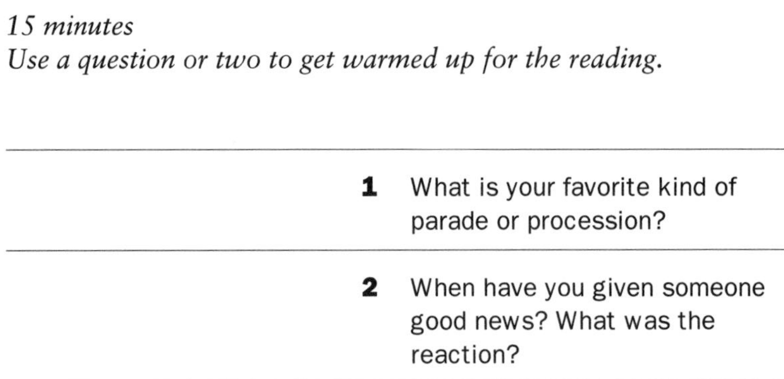

15 minutes
Use a question or two to get warmed up for the reading.

1 What is your favorite kind of parade or procession?

2 When have you given someone good news? What was the reaction?

Opening the Bible

5 minutes
Read the passage aloud. Let individuals take turns. (Suggestion: first speaker—verses 1–2; second speaker—verses 3–5; third speaker—verses 6–8; fourth speaker—verses 9–11; all together—verses 12–15; fifth speaker—verses 27–29.)

The Reading: Isaiah 40:1–15, 27–29

The Prophet's Call

1 Comfort, O comfort my people,
says your God.
2 Speak tenderly to Jerusalem,
and cry to her
that she has served her term,
that her penalty is paid,
that she has received from the Lord's hand
double for all her sins.

3 A voice cries out:
"In the wilderness prepare the way of the Lord,
make straight in the desert a highway for our God.
4 Every valley shall be lifted up,
and every mountain and hill be made low;
the uneven ground shall become level,
and the rough places a plain.
5 Then the glory of the LORD shall be revealed,
and all people shall see it together,
for the mouth of the LORD has spoken."

6 A voice says, "Cry out!"
And I said, "What shall I cry?"
All people are grass,
their constancy is like the flower of the field.
7 The grass withers, the flower fades,
when the breath of the LORD blows upon it;
surely the people are grass.
8 The grass withers, the flower fades;
but the word of our God will stand forever.
9 Get you up to a high mountain,
O Zion, herald of good tidings;
lift up your voice with strength,
O Jerusalem, herald of good tidings,
lift it up, do not fear;
say to the cities of Judah,
"Here is your God!"

10 See, the Lord God comes with might,
and his arm rules for him;
his reward is with him,
and his recompense before him.
11 He will feed his flock like a shepherd;
he will gather the lambs in his arms,
and carry them in his bosom,
and gently lead the mother sheep.

God Can Do What He Promises

12 Who has measured the waters in the hollow of his hand
and marked off the heavens with a span,
enclosed the dust of the earth in a measure,
and weighed the mountains in scales
and the hills in a balance?
13 Who has directed the spirit of the LORD,
or as his counselor has instructed him?
14 Whom did he consult for his enlightenment,
and who taught him the path of justice?
Who taught him knowledge,
and showed him the way of understanding?
15 Even the nations are like a drop from a bucket,
and are accounted as dust on the scales;
see, he takes up the isles like fine dust. . . .

A Response to Those Who Feel Abandoned

27 Why do you say, O Jacob,
and speak, O Israel,
"My way is hidden from the LORD,
and my right is disregarded by my God"?
28 Have you not known? Have you not heard?
The LORD is the everlasting God,
the Creator of the ends of the earth.
He does not faint or grow weary;
his understanding is unsearchable.
29 He gives power to the faint,
and strengthens the powerless.

Questions for Careful Reading

10 minutes
Choose questions according to your interest and time.

1 Is God the only one for whom the highway is to be built (40:3–4)?*

2 What kinds of events will reveal God's "glory" (40:5)?*

3 What answers are implied by the rhetorical questions in 40:12, 13, 14?

4 What attitude toward God lies behind the protest quoted in 40:27?

5 Who are the faint and powerless in 40:29? What are they given the strength to do?*

*It is helpful to try to answer these questions at this point in our reading. But the answers will become clearer as we continue to read Isaiah in future weeks.

A Guide to the Reading

If participants have not read this section already, read it aloud. Otherwise go on to "Questions for Application."

40:1–5. Imagine yourself in Isaiah's place. In a vision you are standing in heaven. God, like an ancient Near Eastern king, is seated on a throne, surrounded by government ministers (compare Job 1:6–12). As you listen, the heavenly courtiers announce that God has decided to reverse the unhappy situation of his people, Israel.

One voice declares God's decree of liberation: "Comfort, comfort my people." God does not merely wish his people to know that he sympathizes with them in their suffering. The "comfort" lies in the news that God is going to act on their behalf (compare 51:3, 12–14). Help is on the way!

A second voice calls for the landscape to be reconfigured into a highway for God (40:3–5, 10). The focus is on God's action; at this point, human cooperation is secondary. The command issues from God, who created all things by a mere word (Genesis 1). The divine decree itself will bring the road into existence.

God is returning to Jerusalem—to the midst of his people. In one sense, he has never been apart from them (if he had, they would have fallen out of existence). But he withdrew his presence in the sense of refraining from blessing them; he let them taste the bitter consequences of their injustices. But now God is coming back, and the whole world will see his glory.

40:6–8. Now a voice addresses the listening prophet: "Cry out! Tell the people that God is coming!"

In the view of the translators of the NRSV, the prophet's response is brief ("What shall I cry?"). But ancient Hebrew did not use quotation marks. Some scholars think Isaiah's response extends to the end of verse 7. In that case, Isaiah is not really asking *what* he should announce. Instead, he counters the command by implying that there is no use in making any announcement to the Israelites. They have shown themselves to be incapable of "constancy." Israel's history has demonstrated that the people do not have a capacity for loyalty; they are unreliable. A lasting relationship between God and these people is no more possible than a lasting relationship between the withering desert wind and fragile wildflowers (compare Psalms 39; 90). Why should God bother speaking to us, Isaiah asks, since we do not take hold of his word? Anyone who has ever seen a marriage or career wrecked by infidelity, abuse, addiction, or irresponsibility will understand Isaiah's reluctance to believe that a new start is possible.

A heavenly voice responds vigorously (40:8). Biblical scholar Claus Westermann comments: "The voice that now speaks does not deny that Israel's circumstances are what the prophet . . . takes them to be. From the human point of view there is nothing more to be done. . . . However, the sheer hopelessness of the situation is confronted with the reality of the word of God." Despite human sin, God *will* resume his relationship with his people.

40:9–11. Jerusalem is pictured as a woman (Zion, addressed in the Hebrew as a woman, is the hill where the ancient city stood). She is told to announce to the surrounding towns that God has achieved a victory and is returning with prisoners and spoils. No battle is described; in a sense, none has occurred. God gains victories without fighting on any battlefield. God simply decrees. God has won the release of the Israelite exiles and is leading them back to the depopulated towns of Judea. A similar announcement of unseen victory over evil will mark Jesus' ministry (Mark 1:15; Luke 10:18).

Isaiah pictures God as a king marching at the head of a victorious column of troops, but could anything look less military than the movement of flocks? The image emphasizes the king's concern for each of his subjects. At a later time, Jesus also would neutralize the military connotations of a parade (John 12:14).

40:12–15. Another possible objection to God's decree is that liberation for Israel is politically and militarily inconceivable. The Babylonian empire blocks Israelite aspirations to freedom. The answer to this skepticism is a magnificent statement of God's sovereignty. No one can measure God or advise God or compare with God in any way. The might of Babylon and its gods are nothing before the ruler of the universe.

40:27–29. God not only asserts his ability to help his people; he also assures them that he will give them strength to cooperate with him. Old Testament scholar Paul Hanson calls these verses "the poetry of empowerment." Of course, to receive God's power, we must believe in it.

Questions for Application

40 minutes
Choose questions according to your interest and time.

1. When has it seemed that God has taken the initiative in your life?

2. Where in your life would you like to experience God's liberating power? Where in the world would you most like to see God's justice? How might you cooperate with God in both of these areas?

3. When do you tend to become discouraged about the possibility of growing closer to God? What is the message of today's reading for you?

4. When have you been the recipient of words of comfort? What did you learn from the experience? In the coming week, how could you be a herald of comfort to someone else?

5 When have you seen the value of speaking tenderly and gently?

6 Using the view of God's glory in this passage (combining 40:5 with 40:11), when have you seen God's glory? Have you ever seen God's glory without recognizing it at the time?

7 Mark quotes Isaiah 40:3 (Mark 1:3). How does reading Isaiah 40 help in understanding Mark 1:1–15?

The most common fear when approaching the formidable journey of Bible reading is that we are not smart enough. . . . Well, trust yourself as a reader. The Bible was not written for scholars but for ordinary people.

Steve Mueller, *The Seeker's Guide to Reading the Bible*

Approach to Prayer

15 minutes
Use this approach—or create your own!

- Have someone read aloud Luke 2:22–28. Then pray aloud together the words that the elderly Simeon speaks when he meets Mary and Joseph with the infant Jesus in the temple (Luke 2:29–32):

Master, now you are dismissing
  your servant in peace,
 according to your word;
for my eyes have seen your
  salvation,
 which you have prepared in
  the presence of all peoples,
a light for revelation to the
  Gentiles
 and for glory to your people
  Israel.

End with a Glory to the Father and an Our Father.

Saints in the Making

Sent to Bring Comfort

This section is a supplement for individual reading.

After traveling from Michigan to visit my daughter, I was sitting by the pool at her apartment complex one evening in Fort Worth, Texas. The night was cool and the water reflected the sparkling lights. I was alone and enjoying the quiet on a very comfortable lounge chair.

Suddenly, God spoke to my heart. "Dean, I want you to take my holy word and my body and blood in the most holy Eucharist into the prisons and jails."

My immediate response was "No, God, I do not want anything to do with this. Lock these people up and leave them there." My attitude was, they are getting just what they deserve.

I wrestled in my heart with God for two weeks. My fear was too great. What if the prisoners I meet get out of prison and come to my house, I asked myself. What if? What if? The questions went through my mind over and over. Yet God had an answer for every doubt and fear I could imagine. St. Peter had to face his fear by stepping out of the boat and walking on the water toward Christ.

The Lord had called me. He came into my heart so strongly that I could not say no. Two weeks later, on that same lounge chair, by that same pool, I surrendered my life, my family, and all my possessions to the Lord. Even if I lost everything, I was going to follow the Lord into the prisons and jails.

That was fourteen years ago. Now when I share with inmates, I tell them that I do not come to them to give them anything of myself. I come to bring them the body and blood of the Lord in the most holy Eucharist and to receive the suffering of Christ through them.

If not for God's calling, I would never go back into a prison or jail. But God has continued to call me to bring his comfort to those who are imprisoned. And "I can do all things through him who strengthens me" (Philippians 4:13).

Dean Hedglen

Week 2

DIVINE LOGIC

Questions to Begin

15 minutes
Use a question or two to get warmed up for the reading.

---

1 When do you find it hard to refrain from saying what's on your mind?

---

2 When have you had something stolen from you? Were you upset? (Are you still upset?)

Opening the Bible

5 minutes
Read the passage aloud. Let individuals take turns reading. (Suggestion: first speaker—42:14–16; second speaker—42:18–20; third speaker—42:21–23; all together—42:24–25; fourth speaker—43:1–3; fifth speaker—44:21–22)

The Reading: Isaiah 42:14–43:3; 44:21–22

God Returns to Action

14 For a long time I have held my peace,
I have kept still and restrained myself;
now I will cry out like a woman in labor,
I will gasp and pant.
15 I will lay waste mountains and hills,
and dry up all their herbage;
I will turn the rivers into islands,
and dry up the pools.
16 I will lead the blind
by a road they do not know,
by paths they have not known
I will guide them.
I will turn the darkness before them into light,
the rough places into level ground. . . .

Which Is Blind?

18 Listen, you that are deaf;
and you that are blind, look up and see!
19 Who is blind but my servant,
or deaf like my messenger whom I send?
Who is blind like my dedicated one,
or blind like the servant of the LORD?
20 He sees many things, but does not observe them;
his ears are open, but he does not hear.
21 The LORD was pleased, for the sake of his righteousness,
to magnify his teaching and make it glorious.
22 But this is a people robbed and plundered,
all of them are trapped in holes
and hidden in prisons;
they have become a prey with no one to rescue,
a spoil with no one to say, "Restore!"
23 Who among you will give heed to this,
who will attend and listen for the time to come?

24 Who gave up Jacob to the spoiler,
and Israel to the robbers?
Was it not the Lord, against whom we have sinned,
in whose ways they would not walk,
and whose law they would not obey?
25 So he poured upon him the heat of his anger
and the fury of war;
it set him on fire all around, but he did not understand;
it burned him, but he did not take it to heart.

Nevertheless—

43:1 But now thus says the Lord,
he who created you, O Jacob,
he who formed you, O Israel:
Do not fear, for I have redeemed you;
I have called you by name, you are mine.
2 When you pass through the waters, I will be with you;
and through the rivers, they shall not overwhelm you;
when you walk through fire you shall not be burned,
and the flame shall not consume you.
3 For I am the LORD your God,
the Holy One of Israel, your Savior. . . .

44:21 Remember these things, O Jacob,
and Israel, for you are my servant;
I formed you, you are my servant;
O Israel, you will not be forgotten by me.
22 I have swept away your transgressions like a cloud,
and your sins like mist;
return to me, for I have redeemed you.

Questions for Careful Reading

10 minutes
Choose questions according to your interest and time.

1 What is the "long time" in 42:14? (You may wish to refer to page 8.)

2 What is the point of the labor imagery in 42:14?

3 In 42:18–25, what does God see? What do the Israelites not see?

4 Verses 42:15–16 echo 40:3–4. What composite picture is formed by putting the two passages together?

5 What general impression of the Israelites' situation do you get from 42:22, 24?

6 What event is referred to in 42:25? (You may wish to consult page 7.)

A Guide to the Reading

If participants have not read this section already, read it aloud. Otherwise go on to "Questions for Application."

Reading the excerpt from chapter 42 is like listening to one side of a phone conversation. We have to figure out what is being said on the other end.

42:14–16. We may suppose that the Israelite exiles have been praying something like Psalm 44:23–24: "Rouse yourself! Why do you sleep, O Lord? Awake, do not cast us off forever! Why do you hide your face? Why do you forget our affliction and oppression?" To a degree, God acknowledges the truth of their complaint; he *has* held back from helping them. But he declares that divine action will now replace inaction as suddenly and violently as the turmoil of labor breaks upon the relative quiet of pregnancy. The image of childbearing does not suggest that God is female any more than the imagery of 42:13 suggests that God is male. God is beyond gender. But every aspect of human life may provide analogies that help us glimpse something of the incomprehensible God.

The imagery of geological upheaval (42:15) symbolizes God's determination to sweep aside the enemies who obstruct his people's march to freedom. Yet the God who can rearrange mountains as if they were living-room furniture will gently take account of each person's limitations and weaknesses (42:16).

42:18–25. Apparently the Israelites have accused God of being blind and deaf to their suffering (as in 40:27). God responds, "Who is blind and deaf? I know all about your situation [see 42:22]. *You* are the blind and deaf ones, because you fail to perceive that it was your exploitations and injustices that brought disaster on you [see 42:18–20]." The Israelites heard God's warnings through prophets and felt his hand in the collapse of their nation. But have they absorbed the lesson that God wished to convey? Verse 42:24 indicates that the message is *beginning* to sink in. Despite this flicker of insight, however, their condition is one of spiritual blindness (42:25). Biblical scholar Walter Brueggemann explains Isaiah's point this way: "The punishment was to produce repentance on the part of Israel. But it did not work! Israel is completely obdurate. . . . Israel did not get it at the moment of the destruction of Jerusalem, but Israel still does not get it two generations later."

Israel's situation seems hopeless. In this case, sin brought disaster, but disaster has not brought wisdom. If the working out of painful consequences for sin through historical cause and effect does not bring people to a repentant understanding of their behavior, what remedy remains?

43:1–3. After the terrible indictment of 42:25, the listener may fear that some new judgment will now befall the discipline-resistant exiles. But in an amazing reversal, there comes forth a declaration of reconciliation. God shows grace to sinners, even to those who fail to recognize their sins. To people so blind to their sins that they don't learn even when their wrongdoing brings the roof down on them, the Creator cries out: "Nevertheless, you are mine! I redeem you from your sins!" To each and every Israelite, God declares, "You belong to me. I will protect you."

44:21–22. We might expect that after we sin, reconciliation with God must originate with us: we must admit our wrongdoing and ask forgiveness. But divine logic is different from human logic. Return to me, *because I have redeemed you,* God declares (44:22). God prepares the way back to him and invites us to walk on it. His word is not "Repent so that I may forgive you" or "Prove you're sorry, and I will have mercy on you." God says, "Come back to me, because I have already come back to you!"

In another passage, God says to the exiles, "You have burdened me with your sins; you have wearied me with your iniquities." Yet he immediately declares, "I, I am He who blots out your transgressions for my own sake, and I will not remember your sins" (43:24–25). Scholar Roger Whybray writes that Isaiah did not regard repentance as a precondition for God's forgiveness; rather it is God's offer of forgiveness that opens the way for our repentance. And how necessary this divine logic is. From the midst of our sins, we could never find our own way back to God. Without God's grace, we might not even wish to make the journey. I can imagine Jesus at lunch with well-known violators of the moral code, using Isaiah's words to support his insistence that God's love reaches out to men and women even before they reach out to God (compare Luke 5:27–32; 15:1–32; 19:1–10).

Questions for Application

40 minutes
Choose questions according to your interest and time.

---

1 When has God seemed inactive, unresponsive, deaf to you? How has this affected your relationship with God? What have you learned through it?

---

2 Have you been failing to respond to someone's request for help? What step could you take to help them?

---

3 Reread 42:18–20, 23–25 and read Matthew 7:3–5. Why is it easier to recognize other people's sins than our own? Why do we sometimes fail to recognize our own patterns of sin?

---

4 What attitudes are important if we are to learn from our mistakes? What is helpful for identifying patterns of selfishness and sin in ourselves?

5 When have you taken the initiative to extend forgiveness to someone who wronged you? When has someone taken that initiative with you? What can be learned from such experiences? To whom might you take the initiative to extend forgiveness?

6 What portion of this week's reading might be helpful to you in preparing for the sacrament of reconciliation?

7 For personal reflection rather than discussion: Where do you need God's grace to enable you to acknowledge some sin and repent? Do you ask God for help?

Work on your listening skills. For promoting an open and sharing atmosphere, nothing that you say will be more important than how well you listen.

Gerald Sigler, *Getting Started: How to Begin a Bible Study Program*

Approach to Prayer

15 minutes
Use this approach—or create your own!

- Ask someone to read aloud Romans 5:6–11 (given below). Pause for silent reflection. Allow any who wish to express a short prayer of any sort. Close together with an Our Father.

While we were still weak, at the right time Christ died for the ungodly. Indeed, rarely will anyone die for a righteous person—though perhaps for a good person someone might actually dare to die. But God proves his love for us in that while we still were sinners Christ died for us. Much more surely then, now that we have been justified by his blood, will we be saved through him from the wrath of God. For if while we were enemies, we were reconciled to God through the death of his Son, much more surely, having been reconciled, will we be saved by his life. But more than that, we even boast in God through our Lord Jesus Christ, through whom we have now received reconciliation.

A Living Tradition

Forgiveness, Repentance, and Baptism

This section is a supplement for individual reading.

Two early Christian teachers who wrote about the book of Isaiah were a bishop named Eusebius and a monk named Jerome. Eusebius was bishop of Caesarea, on the coast of present-day Israel. His book about Isaiah, written around the year 325, was later lost for centuries. In the 1930s, someone realized that the extensive notes written in the margins of an old copy of the Bible were actually the bulk of Eusebius's Isaiah commentary.

Jerome was rare among early Christian biblical scholars: he moved from Italy to the Holy Land and studied Hebrew. Jerome read Eusebius's commentary on Isaiah and wrote his own commentary around 410. Here the two ancient scholars comment on God's declarations of forgiveness in Isaiah.

Eusebius on Isaiah 44:21–22:

In order to encourage the people to get moving toward repentance, God proclaims that if they return to him he has already granted them forgiveness of their sins. That is why he says, "I *have swept away*"—not "I *will sweep away*—your transgressions like a cloud."

Jerome on Isaiah 43:24–25:

"You, Jacob and Israel, have wearied me with your sins, and I can hardly bear the weight of your iniquity," the Lord declares. . . . "But I, because of myself, because I am compassionate and patient and full of mercies, I will obliterate all your evil deeds with the sprinkling of the blood of the new covenant. Terminating the contract of your enslavement to sin that was written down of old, I will no longer keep any record of your sins and, if you are willing to believe, I am going to forgive your sins in baptism."

Week 3

Remember! Forget!

Questions to Begin

15 minutes
Use a question or two to get warmed up for the reading.

---

1 How many generations back can you trace your family?

---

2 What is the most valuable thing you learned from your father or mother or from some other older member of your family?

---

3 Describe one of the nicest surprises you ever received or prepared for someone else.

Opening the Bible

5 minutes
Read the passage aloud. Let individuals take turns reading. (Suggestion: first speaker—43:4–7; second speaker—43:14–17; third speaker—43:18–21; fourth speaker—51:1–2; fifth speaker—51:3.)

The Reading: Isaiah 43:4–7, 14–21; 51:1–3

God Will Bring the Exiles Home

4 Because you are precious in my sight,
and honored, and I love you,
I give people in return for you,
nations in exchange for your life.
5 Do not fear, for I am with you;
I will bring your offspring from the east,
and from the west I will gather you;
6 I will say to the north, "Give them up,"
and to the south, "Do not withhold;
bring my sons from far away
and my daughters from the end of the earth—
7 everyone who is called by my name,
whom I created for my glory,
whom I formed and made." . . .

It Will Be Like the Exodus from Egypt

14 Thus says the Lord,
your Redeemer, the Holy One of Israel:
For your sake I will send to Babylon
and break down all the bars,
and the shouting of the Chaldeans will be turned to lamentation.
15 I am the Lord, your Holy One,
the Creator of Israel, your King.
16 Thus says the Lord,
who makes a way in the sea,
a path in the mighty waters,
17 who brings out chariot and horse,
army and warrior;
they lie down, they cannot rise,
they are extinguished, quenched like a wick:
18 Do not remember the former things,
or consider the things of old.
19 I am about to do a new thing;
now it springs forth, do you not perceive it?

I will make a way in the wilderness
    and rivers in the desert.
20 The wild animals will honor me,
    the jackals and the ostriches;
for I give water in the wilderness,
    rivers in the desert,
to give drink to my chosen people,
21 the people whom I formed for myself
so that they might declare my praise. . . .

Chips, Remember Your Old Block!

51:1 Listen to me, you that pursue righteousness,
    you that seek the Lord.
Look to the rock from which you were hewn,
    and to the quarry from which you were dug.
2 Look to Abraham your father
    and to Sarah who bore you;
for he was but one when I called him,
    but I blessed him and made him many.
3 For the LORD will comfort Zion;
    he will comfort all her waste places,
and will make her wilderness like Eden,
    her desert like the garden of the LORD;
joy and gladness will be found in her,
    thanksgiving and the voice of song.

Questions for Careful Reading

10 minutes
Choose questions according to your interest and time.

1 To whom does "you" and "your" refer in 43:5 and 43:14? Does 40:9 help in answering this question?

2 God declares that he is "with" the Israelites (43:5; compare 43:2). From the context, what does this statement mean? (How might this usage help to explain the meaning of the liturgical greeting "The Lord be with you"?)

3 What kind of shouting seems to be meant in 43:14?

4 Abraham is memorable because in extreme old age he became the ancestor of an entire nation (51:2). Why is Sarah memorable? (See Genesis 11:30; 18:9–15.)

5 What is the parallel between the situation of Abraham and Sarah and that of the Israelites to whom God is speaking in 51:1–3?

A Guide to the Reading

If participants have not read this section already, read it aloud. Otherwise go on to "Questions for Application."

43:4–7. God will gather the exiles and bring them back to Jerusalem. Isaiah's statement that God values them more than other people should not be taken to mean that he thinks they have greater intrinsic dignity or worth. As Walter Brueggemann observes, it expresses God's "treasuring Israel in an extreme way." Isaiah calls God "Redeemer" (43:14). Yet while a redeemer frees someone or something by paying a ransom, God frees without exchange. Jesus redeemed us by his death, but his act did not involve paying anyone anything.

The political and military leaders of Babylon would have been astonished to hear that God was concerned about the seemingly insignificant Israelite exiles. God shows a "preferential love" for people who suffer impoverishment through exile or other causes. It is a preference that we are called to imitate (see the *Catechism of the Catholic Church,* sections 2444, 2448).

In Jesus' preaching, the return of the Jewish exiles becomes an image of the gathering of all humanity into God's kingdom. Jesus speaks of God's kingdom as a banquet to which people come from every direction (Luke 13:29; compare 43:5–7). We begin to taste this banquet in the Eucharist. If the Eucharist reflects a meal to which all are invited, especially those who are in distress, then living a life imbued with the Eucharist involves demonstrating a practical concern for the suffering of other people, especially those who are in great need. Isaiah speaks of God's glory being reflected in the exiles' return to a safe, secure, and holy life (43:5–7). If we wish to live for God's glory, we will devote ourselves to securing such a life for the exiles and refugees of our own day.

43:14–21; 51:1–3. God reminds the exiles of what he has done for them as a people (43:14–17). The imagery brings to mind God's rescue of their ancestors from Egypt. At that time God brought the Israelites to safety through water (43:16; Exodus 14:26–31). God reminds their descendants of that exodus in order to stir their hope that he will do something similar for them.

The similarity between what God did for the Israelites in the past and what he now intends to do highlights an aspect of God's dealings with the human race. God is executing a plan throughout history. Every phase of his activity bears his hallmarks:

God typically intervenes on behalf of the poor and oppressed; his actions are characteristically lavish (like his creation of the garden of Eden—51:3) and life-giving (like his gift of many descendants to Abraham and Sarah—51:1–2). Thus God's actions in successive ages bear a resemblance to one another. His actions in one age become models for later deeds.

Yet, having stirred the exiles' faith by pointing to God's previous rescue of Israel, Isaiah wheels around and tells them to *forget* what God has done in the past! God's rescue of the Jews from Babylon (43:14; "Chaldeans" are Babylonians) will be so much more magnificent than the exodus from Egypt that the two events will be hardly comparable (43:18–19). After the exodus from Egypt, God provided his people with water at stopping places here and there in the wilderness (Exodus 17:1–7; Numbers 20:1–13); in the new exodus, he will send rivers flowing through the desert (43:19).

The Israelites may have been complaining that God cares less for them than he did for their ancestors. God's reply, in effect, is "Stop mournfully looking back and clinging to the past, and open your minds to the fact that a new, miraculous act of God lies ahead of you!" (Claus Westermann). Certainly faith remembers what God has done. But it also believes that God remains powerfully present in the world today.

While God's interaction with humanity continues to unfold according to a pattern, each new stage holds surprises. The coming of God's Son surpassed the return from exile (the return was a rather low-key affair—see page 78). Jesus' death and resurrection was the ultimate exodus—a rescue from the forces of sin and death itself. It is easy to imagine Paul applying this reading in Isaiah to the way that God's gift of life through Jesus surpassed even his gift of life through the Torah (compare Philippians 3:4–11). And even Jesus' earthly life will be surpassed by the splendor of the full coming of God's kingdom. Then, like buds opening into blossoms, all signs of God's presence will give way to the full reality they signified. God's complete, joyous rule over every creature and every heart will then be publicly revealed (Philippians 2:9–11).

Questions for Application

40 minutes
Choose questions according to your interest and time.

---

1 In society today, whose lives are regarded as less precious than others'? What value system underlies this unequal view? How does this system of values compare with the gospel?

---

2 God's concern for the scattered Israelites stands as an image of his concern for the many people today who have been forcibly uprooted from their homes and homelands. Who are the displaced persons, exiles, and refugees of the world today? Do any live in your town? What kind of assistance do they need? What can you do to help?

---

3 In what ways do members of the community with which you celebrate the Eucharist show God's love to people who suffer poverty and oppression? What effort could you make to help out?

4 Do you look back longingly to Jesus' years on earth? to days when the Church seemed more vibrant or united? to the saints of earlier centuries? to the good things of the past? What does the reading from Isaiah say about this attitude?

5 On the other hand, what past experiences of God's love strengthen your faith in him today?

A participant in a Bible study group needs to do his or her homework, reading and reflecting on the week's assignment. But group study allows each participant to profit from the insights of other members.

George Martin, *How to Get Started Reading the Bible*

Approach to Prayer

15 minutes
Use this approach—or create your own!

- Pray Psalm 139 as an expression of wonder and thanks for each human person at every stage of life. End with an Our Father as a prayer for God's justice to come to those in the world who are weak and most in need of his help.

Saints in the Making

This section is a supplement for individual reading.

"I am about to do a new thing;
  now it springs forth, do you not perceive it?" (Isaiah 43:19)

Karen Bussey, of Lansing, Michigan, was a social worker who cared for hospice patients. From her first day on the job, she saw people who were going through their terminal illness without family or friends to give them the care they needed. "I talked with many administrators about the problem," Karen recalls, "but I did not assume it was my responsibility to do something about it." When Karen began to spend more time in daily prayer, however, she found growing within her a desire to do something for dying people who did not have adequate care.

"My background was as a clinical social worker," she says. "I did not have the training needed to run an organization. I didn't have funds or a house or connections with influential people that would enable me to pull something together. And I knew that it is not God's plan for you to take care of every need you see. But I felt that God was telling me, 'You do something.'" So she began.

"My profession had taught me to apply resources to the most people possible. But I remembered Mother Teresa's statement that if she had not picked up the first person off the street, she never would have started." So Karen began by moving in with a person who was dying, to help her through her final days.

When he heard of Karen's intentions, the Catholic bishop of Lansing offered her the use of a house, rent-free. The offer came close to the time of Mother Teresa's death, so Karen decided to call the hospice the Mother Teresa House for the Care of the Terminally Ill. It opened in September 1998.

Since then, Karen has recruited and trained a team of volunteers. Together they provide care without charge to guests who come to spend their last days in an atmosphere of peace and reconciliation. Through Karen's leadership, the Mother Teresa House has become an opportunity for people who are suffering and lonely to experience the message that God communicated centuries ago through the prophet Isaiah: "You are precious in my sight, and honored, and I love you" (Isaiah 43:4).

Promises Overflowing

If Isaiah had shaped his messages into a more journalistic form, crowding them with realistic details of God's impending actions, they might make more satisfying reading for historians today. But then his prophecies might have seemed like an ancient relic, from which we would have a hard time deriving any meaning for our situation today. In calling Isaiah to be his spokesman, however, God chose a poet rather than a newspaper reporter. Isaiah spoke in poetic form. And we may be glad that he did, for poems, like music, have a peculiar ability to leap over cultural barriers and speak to us directly, even when we are somewhat unfamiliar with the time and place in which they originated. One of the finest examples of Isaiah's poetic art, and of his poems' capacity to address us twenty-five centuries after he wrote, is the set of divine promises and reassurances in chapter 49.

8 Thus says the Lord:
In a time of favor I have answered you,
on a day of salvation I have helped you;
I have kept you and given you
as a covenant to the people, . . .
9 saying to the prisoners, "Come out,"
to those who are in darkness, "Show yourselves."
They shall feed along the ways,
on all the bare heights shall be their pasture;
10 they shall not hunger or thirst,
neither scorching wind nor sun shall strike them down,
for he who has pity on them will lead them,
and by springs of water will guide them.
11 And I will turn all my mountains into a road,
and my highways shall be raised up.
12 Lo, these shall come from far away,
and lo, these from the north and from the west,
and these from the land of Syene.

13 Sing for joy, O heavens, and exult, O earth;
break forth, O mountains, into singing!
For the LORD has comforted his people,
and will have compassion on his suffering ones.

14 But Zion said, "The Lord has forsaken me,
my Lord has forgotten me."
15 Can a woman forget her nursing child,
or show no compassion for the child of her womb?
Even these may forget,
yet I will not forget you.
16 See, I have inscribed you on the palms of my hands;
your walls are continually before me.
17 Your builders outdo your destroyers,
and those who laid you waste go away from you.
18 Lift up your eyes all around and see;
they all gather, they come to you.
As I live, says the Lord,
you shall put all of them on like an ornament,
and like a bride you shall bind them on.

19 Surely your waste and your desolate places
and your devastated land—
surely now you will be too crowded for your inhabitants,
and those who swallowed you up will be far away.
20 The children born in the time of your bereavement
will yet say in your hearing:
"The place is too crowded for me;
make room for me to settle."
21 Then you will say in your heart,
"Who has borne me these?
I was bereaved and barren,
exiled and put away—
so who has reared these?
I was left all alone—
where then have these come from?"

Isaiah's words supply much food for pondering and praying. Which parts of this poem seem to best express God's message to you? What can you do to remember these words? What sort of response do Isaiah's words invite you to make?

Week 4

Good News That's Hard to Take

Questions to Begin

15 minutes
Use a question or two to get warmed up for the reading.

---

1 When has going through a door or crossing a threshold been a memorable occasion in your life?

---

2 Looking back, when has it been a good thing that you were not able to see into the future?

Opening the Bible

5 minutes
Read the passage aloud. Let individuals take turns reading. (Suggestion: first reader—44:24–28; second reader—45:1–6; third reader—45:9; fourth reader—45:10; fifth reader—45:11–13.)

The Reading: Isaiah 44:24–45:13

God, the Ruler of History

24 Thus says the Lord, your Redeemer,
who formed you in the womb:
I am the Lord, who made all things,
who alone stretched out the heavens,
who by myself spread out the earth;
25 who frustrates the omens of liars,
and makes fools of diviners;
who turns back the wise,
and makes their knowledge foolish;
26 who confirms the word of his servant,
and fulfills the prediction of his messengers;
who says of Jerusalem, "It shall be inhabited,"
and of the cities of Judah, "They shall be rebuilt,
and I will raise up their ruins";
27 who says to the deep, "Be dry—
I will dry up your rivers";
28 who says of Cyrus, "He is my shepherd,
and he shall carry out all my purpose";
and who says of Jerusalem, "It shall be rebuilt,"
and of the temple, "Your foundation shall be laid."

Surprise, Surprise!

45:1 Thus says the LORD to his anointed, to Cyrus,
whose right hand I have grasped
to subdue nations before him
and strip kings of their robes,
to open doors before him—
and the gates shall not be closed:
2 I will go before you
and level the mountains,
I will break in pieces the doors of bronze
and cut through the bars of iron,
3 I will give you the treasures of darkness
and riches hidden in secret places,

so that you may know that it is I, the Lord,
the God of Israel, who call you by your name.
4 For the sake of my servant Jacob,
and Israel my chosen,
I call you by your name,
I surname you, though you do not know me.
5 I am the LORD, and there is no other;
besides me there is no god.
I arm you, though you do not know me,
6 so that they may know, from the rising of the sun
and from the west, that there is no one besides me;
I am the LORD, and there is no other. . . .

Can Creatures Advise God?

9 Woe to you who strive with your Maker,
earthen vessels with the potter!
Does the clay say to the one who fashions it, "What are you making"?
or "Your work has no handles"?
10 Woe to anyone who says to a father, "What are you begetting?"
or to a woman, "With what are you in labor?"
11 Thus says the LORD,
the Holy One of Israel, and its Maker:
Will you question me about my children,
or command me concerning the work of my hands?
12 I made the earth,
and created humankind upon it;
it was my hands that stretched out the heavens,
and I commanded all their host.
13 I have aroused Cyrus in righteousness,
and I will make all his paths straight;
he shall build my city
and set my exiles free.

Questions for Careful Reading

10 minutes
Choose questions according to your interest and time.

1 Verses 24 through 28 of chapter 44 simply introduce the message that begins with 45:1. What purpose does this introduction serve? Why is it so long?

2 Verse 44:25 puts "the wise" in the same category as omen interpreters and liars. What kind of wisdom do these people have? How does it differ from true wisdom?

3 What ends will God achieve through Cyrus?

4 Read 45:9–11. What response do you suppose the Israelites are making to God's decision to use Cyrus?

5 What is the meaning of the English word *host*? (If you're stumped, check the dictionary for help.) What does it refer to in 45:12?

6 The fulfillment of his prophets' predictions shows that God is Lord of history (44:24–26). Isaiah predicts that Cyrus will conquer Babylon (45:1–3). When this happens, who will recognize it as a demonstration of God's lordship? Who won't?

A Guide to the Reading

If participants have not read this section already, read it aloud. Otherwise go on to "Questions for Application."

44:24–28. God reminds the Israelites that he rules over history. He supports his assertion by pointing to his ability to speak knowledgeably about upcoming events (44:26). The most recent, if painful, example of this divine foresight was the preaching of Israelite prophets: by God's inspiration they warned Jerusalem of its impending destruction. By contrast, the gods of other religions are unable to chart the course of world events. Babylonian and Assyrian religion had prophets of a sort—"diviners" and "liars" (the Hebrew word may be a technical term for fortune-tellers). But archaeologists have never found any record of *those* prophets alerting *their* rulers that their regimes were about to collapse.

Once again, God is about to demonstrate his rule over history (45:6). Just at the point when the Israelites are about to disappear as a people, God will intervene to sustain them. Their continued existence will be evidence that there truly is a God at work in the world, a God whose activity spans the ages. Similarly, the survival and growth of the Church, despite changing circumstances and the failings of its human members, testifies to the presence of this millennia-spanning God.

Isaiah's announcement that God is about to restore the Israelites' fortunes has caught them off guard. But at least this surprising news is of the almost-too-good-to-be-true variety. Now comes a less welcome surprise. Isaiah names the person through whom God is going to liberate them. It is Cyrus the Persian! (44:28; see page 78.)

45:1–6. The careful Israelite listener might have noticed that Isaiah has so far made no mention of the Israelite monarchy or the royal family of David. There has been no hint that the Israelites' liberation will be achieved by an Israelite king (for example, 40:9–11). Rather, Isaiah has declared that Israel's king is the Lord (43:15; 44:6). *What about David?* the listener may be wondering. The answer now begins to emerge. It seems that David's dynasty—indeed, the whole notion of kingship in Israel—is being retired.

Isaiah uses terms employed in the enthronement of kings (45:1–4; compare Psalm 2). The mention of Jerusalem would bring the Davidic kings to mind, for the descendants of David were anointed as kings of Jerusalem. Yet now there is to be a new king for Jerusalem, a kind of new David, who is not a descendant of David. This new king over Israel is not even a worshiper of the God of Israel ("You do not know me," God tells Cyrus—45:4, 5). *What is going on here?* the Israelite audience must have wondered.

For centuries God used the Israelite monarchy, with its administrative machinery and armed forces, to stabilize and protect the life of his people. But with kingship came power politics, intrigues, a lavish lifestyle, and corruption, eroding the justice and mercy that were supposed to characterize God's people. (Some in Israel had foreseen this outcome—1 Samuel 8:10–18.) Now, Isaiah believes, God will dispense with kingship in Israel. His people can be a community of justice and peace, bearing witness to God's faithfulness and mercy, without political power. The duties of maintaining order and protecting the public that God formerly entrusted to the family of David will be assigned to a foreigner.

What about God's promise to David of unending rule (2 Samuel 7:4–17)? Is the promise nullified? Isaiah later indicates that God's promise of faithfulness to David will be fulfilled to the whole people of Israel (55:3–5). Later it will be fulfilled in a special way to a descendant of David who will be a very different kind of king: Jesus of Nazareth (Luke 1:32–33; Romans 1:3–4). He will rule by bearing witness to God's love (John 18:33–37)—and will rule not only Israel but also the world.

45:9–13. Apparently the announcement that Cyrus will be king over Israel has not gone over well. In response to this negative reaction, voices (perhaps in the heavenly court—compare 40:1) uphold God's plan. They do not defend the decree but simply proclaim God's sovereignty. One should not interfere with God's plans any more than one should interrogate a woman in childbirth or a couple having sexual relations (45:10). Klaus Baltzer paraphrases thus: "Why was a Persian of all people needed to bring about salvation? The answer is: God is free in his resolves." We may be reminded of Job. He desired to wrest explanations from God, but God declined to have an argument with him—although he did not object to Job raising his questions (Job 42:7).

Questions for Application

40 minutes
Choose questions according to your interest and time.

---

1 How does a person's experience of God's presence and action strengthen his or her trust in God? Might such experiences also *limit* a person's expectations for how God may yet work in his or her life?

---

2 Are you willing to let God work in your life in new ways? Where might God be calling you to make a difficult change?

---

3 When have you discovered that you could live without someone or something you had considered essential for your happiness? How has the experience affected you?

---

4 When has an uncomfortable situation at home or at work been the setting in which God acted in your life in a new way?

5 When have you argued with God about the ways things have happened in the world? in your life? What resolution did you arrive at?

6 Reread 45:9. What aspects of God's plans for our lives surpass our human understanding?

7 In this reading, God is called "the Holy One" (45:11). What does it mean to say that God is holy? What does it mean for you to be a holy person?

Try to place yourself in the "skin" of Bible characters, identifying with them and their emotions, yearnings, hurts, concerns, difficulties, joys.

Oletta Wald, *The Joy of Discovery in Bible Study*

Approach to Prayer

15 minutes
Use this approach—or create your own!

- Pray this prayer together. End with an Our Father.

  Father, you have created a world filled with change, and each blessing that you give in this world remains only for a while. At times you show your love through abundant gifts; at other times you remove your gifts in order to reveal your love more deeply. In whatever way you choose to show your love, Father, you are to be praised. But your ways are sometimes difficult to welcome, so please deepen our trust in your wisdom and faithfulness. Your love is the great constant in our lives.

Saints in the Making

Learning to Be Pro-life

This section is a supplement for individual reading.

In Isaiah we see a pattern in God's dealings with Israel: a disastrous loss is followed by a restoration that does not restore all that was lost yet becomes a framework for a new phase of God's activity. The pattern repeats itself, not only on the macro level of nations but also on the micro level of communities and individuals. The Franciscan Brothers of Peace, in St. Paul, Minnesota, have experienced it.

In the 1980s, a handful of young men who were heavily involved in political and educational pro-life activities, including civil disobedience, felt drawn to live and pray together. At first they simply called themselves "the brothers." To others they were known as "the pro-life brothers." They were attracted to St. Francis of Assisi and his way of living the gospel. With the blessing of the Catholic archbishop, the group became officially established as a Franciscan association.

In 1991, one of the founders of the group, thirty-two-year-old Michael Gaworski, contracted a severe case of pneumonia. One night, the sickness caused him to go into cardiac arrest. Paramedics revived him, but for days he hovered near death in an intensive care unit of a hospital. Eventually, Michael's condition stabilized, and the brothers brought him home. But there was no return to the way life had been before. Michael had suffered severe brain damage. He seemed aware and alert but was unable to speak or move his body. With the help of medical professionals, the brothers began to care for him around the clock.

Over the years since then, the Franciscan Brothers of Peace have learned much about the difficulty and joy of being pro-life. They have faced opposition from some health-care professionals who sought to persuade them not to give Michael full care. They have learned more about Jesus' identification with the weak and suffering. As they have reshaped their community to provide Michael with long-term care, they have discovered that even a totally disabled person can continue to play a part in a community and, indeed, can be a spur to conversion and a reminder of Jesus' presence among his followers.

Songs of a Suffering Servant

We are about to read one of the most mysterious and important sections of Scripture, and some words of introduction are in order. At several places, Isaiah speaks of an extraordinary servant of God. This servant will proclaim God's word like a prophet, but his mission will go beyond speaking. The servant will suffer and die, and by doing so he will bring about a change in the relationship between God and the Jews and, indeed, between God and other peoples. We are about to read the fourth, climactic Servant Song, sometimes called the Suffering Servant Song. The others are 42:1–4; 49:1–6; and 50:4–9. The best preparation for our target reading from Isaiah in week 5 is to read these earlier (short!) Servant Songs.

The Servant Songs deal with an issue that has already emerged in our readings from Isaiah. Humans lack "constancy" (40:6). Our darker tendencies lead us off the path of peace and into conflict with one another. Even when God allows our sins to have painful consequences, we are slow to recognize our failings (42:18–25). We become locked in a cycle of sin, painful consequences, and partial repentance. How can the cycle ever be broken? How can we ever attain a steady, lasting relationship with God? How can we be people who cling to God and consistently treat others with justice and faithfulness?

The prophets Jeremiah and Ezekiel wrestled with this question and came to the conviction that God would make a change within people. As Jeremiah put it, God would write his laws on our hearts (Jeremiah 31:31–34). In Ezekiel's terms, God would replace our stony hearts with hearts of flesh (Ezekiel 36:26). But how would God accomplish the change within us? Isaiah's Servant Songs give us an insight into God's plan: God will use a servant who dedicates himself to God's will so completely that he takes our sins and their consequences on himself in order to remove them.

Isaiah's portrait of the servant is shadowy, indistinct. The servant will be empowered by God; he will be gentle; he will bring justice (42:1–4). He will experience failure, but God will uphold him. His mission will extend beyond Israel to all the nations of the world (49:1–6). He will listen carefully to God and will speak God's word, even when this brings him scorn and abuse (50:4–9). In the fourth poem, which we are about to read, we discover that the servant's sufferings are great, even lifelong, and lead to a disgraceful death. Yet through his acceptance of the suffering involved in his mission, he will bring about a change in sinful human beings (52:13–53:12).

A central question in interpreting the Servant Songs is who does Isaiah conceive the servant to be? A first, simple answer is "Israel." In the Old Testament, the people of Israel are sometimes called God's "servant" (44:21). In fact, at one point the servant is explicitly identified as Israel (49:3). If the servant symbolizes the people of Israel, the message of the Servant Songs might be that God is assigning a task to his people that entails suffering for them but will be life-giving for the world. In many ways, this is a reasonable interpretation. But identifying the servant as Israel does not completely solve the puzzle of his identity. The servant cannot simply *be* Israel, because he is told to bring God's word *to* Israel (49:5–6). In addition, some of the poems speak of the servant in terms that suit an individual rather than a group (49:1; 53:9).

According to another theory, the servant is the prophet Isaiah. The servant sometimes speaks in the first person, and in the prophetic writings "I" and "me" statements that do not refer to anyone else refer to the prophet himself. The second and third Servant Songs speak in the first person. For example, "The Lord called me before I was born" (49:1) and "The Lord God has opened my ear" (50:5). A problem for this interpretation arises with the fourth song: it speaks about the servant after his death and so could not have been written by Isaiah. But, according to this theory, the fourth Servant Song may have been written about Isaiah by his disciples. If we take the servant to be Isaiah, then the servant is a prophetic figure who stands in the line of the prophetic leaders of Israel, beginning with Moses, whose assignments to bring God's word to his people involved suffering. Yet, again, while there may well be a connection between the servant and Isaiah, this is not a perfect explanation either, for the servant's mission exceeds that of any prophet. A prophet might suffer in solidarity with other people. But the servant not only suffers with others; his death is "an offering for sin" (53:10).

Some scholars suggest that the servant's identity is deliberately obscure. Thus, through the Servant Songs, Isaiah spoke of someone whose identity could not yet be clearly perceived. Isaiah sketched a transaction between God and people that could not yet be fully expressed.

It seems that there are elements of truth in all three views, and they are not mutually exclusive.

Whoever Isaiah's audience thought the servant was, the Servant Songs would have held a powerful message for them. Isaiah had announced that God intended to use a Persian rather than an Israelite king to restore their fortunes. This would force them to rethink their concept of themselves. If Cyrus was to be their king, they would have to embrace a concept of themselves as a people who lacked the satisfactions of political power. Now the image of the suffering servant pointed them toward an even more profound change in their self-understanding. If Cyrus represented a shift of political power away from Israel, the servant represented an inversion of the very notion of power. For what is power in the servant's ministry? The power given to the servant is the power to listen to God and convey God's word, the power to suffer with sinners and for sinners (50:4–9; 53). By worldly standards, this behavior seems weak and ineffectual. But the Servant Songs indicate that it is precisely through such weakness, willingly embraced, that God will bring life and wholeness to men and women (compare 1 Corinthians 1:18–25). Isaiah's listeners would have to ask themselves whether they wanted this kind of power. We must ask the same question of ourselves.

There is a further question about the meaning of the suffering servant. Did Isaiah's Servant Songs foretell the ministry, death, and resurrection of Jesus? The answer is both no and yes. In order to grasp this paradox, it is important to remember that Scripture has dual authorship: there is the human author and the divine one. The human author's scope of vision is much smaller than that of the divine author. Consequently, the human author may be limited in his or her understanding of the meaning that God wishes to convey. God's meaning in a certain passage in Scripture may extend beyond the human author's meaning, although the extension may not become apparent until a later stage of the unfolding of his plans.

It is unlikely that Isaiah, writing in the fifth century before Christ, saw the life and death of Jesus of Nazareth in his mind's eye and thus intended to describe it. He intended to convey to the Jews of his day a message that God had entrusted to him for them in their circumstances. At the same time, Isaiah's prophecies of the servant do speak of Jesus, for God filled Isaiah with intimations of God's action that would not be completely actualized until the coming of his Son. The Servant Songs communicated the idea that God would change people's relationship with him through a human person's obedient suffering, and this idea was fully realized only in Jesus.

Thus we read Isaiah's Servant Songs on two levels. On one level, we strive to understand what Isaiah was saying to his contemporaries—and then seek to apply this message to our own lives. On a second level, we explore how these poems give us insight into the purpose of Jesus' mission on earth—and then reflect on how this insight can deepen our response to him.

It is not certain that Jesus himself made extensive use of the Servant Songs in explaining himself to his disciples. He explicitly quotes these poems only once (Luke 22:37), although he may allude to them on other occasions. But New Testament authors clearly read the Servant Songs on the "second level" and perceive their reference to Jesus (Matthew 8:17; 12:18–21; Acts 8:32–33; 1 Peter 2:22).

Week 5

By Failure He Succeeds

Questions to Begin

15 minutes
Use a question or two to get warmed up for the reading.

1 Describe someone you know who seemed unlikely to succeed but then accomplished something significant.

2 When things do not go well at your job or at home, do you tend to keep quiet about the problems or to speak up?

Opening the Bible

5 minutes
Read the passage aloud. Let individuals take turns reading. (Suggestion: first speaker—52:13–15; all together—53:1; second speaker—53:2–3; third speaker—53:4–6; fourth speaker—53:7–9; fifth speaker—53:10; first speaker—53:11–12.)

The Reading: Isaiah 52:13–53:12

An Astonishing Reversal

13 See, my servant shall prosper;
he shall be exalted and lifted up,
and shall be very high.
14 Just as there were many who were astonished at him
—so marred was his appearance, beyond human semblance,
and his form beyond that of mortals—
15 so he shall startle many nations;
kings shall shut their mouths because of him;
for that which had not been told them they shall see,
and that which they had not heard they shall contemplate.

A Discussion about the Servant

53:1 Who has believed what we have heard?
And to whom has the arm of the LORD been revealed?
2 For he grew up before him like a young plant,
and like a root out of dry ground;
he had no form or majesty that we should look at him,
nothing in his appearance that we should desire him.
3 He was despised and rejected by others;
a man of suffering and acquainted with infirmity;
and as one from whom others hide their faces
he was despised, and we held him of no account.

4 Surely he has borne our infirmities
and carried our diseases;
yet we accounted him stricken,
struck down by God, and afflicted.
5 But he was wounded for our transgressions,
crushed for our iniquities;
upon him was the punishment that made us whole,
and by his bruises we are healed.
6 All we like sheep have gone astray;
we have all turned to our own way,

and the Lord has laid on him
the iniquity of us all.

7 He was oppressed, and he was afflicted,
yet he did not open his mouth;
like a lamb that is led to the slaughter,
and like a sheep that before its shearers is silent,
so he did not open his mouth.
8 By a perversion of justice he was taken away.
Who could have imagined his future?
For he was cut off from the land of the living,
stricken for the transgression of my people.
9 They made his grave with the wicked
and his tomb with the rich,
although he had done no violence,
and there was no deceit in his mouth.

10 Yet it was the will of the LORD to crush him with pain.
When you make his life an offering for sin,
he shall see his offspring, and shall prolong his days;
through him the will of the LORD shall prosper.
11 Out of his anguish he shall see light;
he shall find satisfaction through his knowledge.

God Has the Last Word

The righteous one, my servant, shall make many righteous,
and he shall bear their iniquities.
12 Therefore I will allot him a portion with the great,
and he shall divide the spoil with the strong;
because he poured out himself to death,
and was numbered with the transgressors;
yet he bore the sin of many,
and made intercession for the transgressors.

Questions for Careful Reading

10 minutes
Choose questions according to your interest and time.

1 Who seems to be speaking in 52:13? in 53:11–12?

2 Who seems to be speaking in the rest of this reading? (There is no one certain answer.)

3 What do 53:2–4 suggest about how the speakers related to the servant during his earthly life?

4 Is there any sign of change in the onlookers' view of the servant during his earthly life?

5 Is it possible to detect what ultimately changed the onlookers' view of the servant? Cite particular statements in the text.

A Guide to the Reading

If participants have not read this section already, read it aloud. Otherwise go on to "Questions for Application."

At the beginning and the end of this scene, God makes a declaration about his servant (52:13–15; 53:11–12). In between, we hear other voices—perhaps members of the heavenly court are speaking, as they did in chapter 40 (40:1). Some of these speakers describe the servant's appearance during his earthly life (53:2–3, 7). Others express a new understanding of him that they have attained (53:4–6, 10, and the first half of verse 11).

52:13–15. God points to the servant, who is entering the heavenly court. His words can be translated: "Look there: my servant begins to succeed; he ascends, he is raised up and exalted." God announces that he has transformed his servant's humiliation into triumph; he has used human suffering to achieve a great victory.

53:1. The meaning of this unexpected reversal of fortunes is yet to be explained, but figures in the heavenly court express their total astonishment at the way God's power has worked through human weakness. An incomprehensible achievement!

53:2–3. Other personages recall the apparent insignificance of the servant's life. He was disfigured by suffering (52:14). In Old Testament times, physical beauty was regarded as God's blessing. The servant's pain-distorted face thus seemed to indicate that he lacked God's blessing. Indeed, his suffering was so severe that people turned away from him, appalled at his apparent abandonment by God. "We accounted him stricken, struck down by God" (53:4). Old Testament scholar Claus Westermann writes, "For the ancient world, this attitude was the orthodox, correct, indeed the devout one. Suffering as such indicated God's smiting and his wrath." It was inconceivable that a person so rejected by God could actually be the agent through whom God was carrying out his plans. Is it any easier to comprehend today?

53:4–6. Other voices speak of the act of redemption mysteriously accomplished through the servant's suffering. Isaiah has emphasized that God's forgiveness precedes his people's repentance (44:22). Now an act of redemption opens the way for repentance. The means of redemption—the servant's suffering—leads sinners to recognize their sins. They have come to recognize their sins by watching the innocent servant share in the punishment their sins deserved.

The Hebrew translation "He was wounded for our transgressions" could mean "he suffered *as a consequence of* our sins." This could suggest that the servant simply shared the painful lot of those to whom he was sent. Yet the servant does more than show solidarity with sinful people: "Upon him was the punishment that made us whole, and by his bruises we are healed" (53:5). These words would be fully realized centuries later in Jesus. Jesus would stand among sinners at his baptism in the Jordan River. Yet he would do more than express solidarity with us in our sins. By his suffering and death, Jesus would bring about a change in us and in our relationship with God.

53:7–9. The servant's burial with the wicked shows that he was unrecognized as God's agent right to the end of his earthly existence. From the beginning to the end of his life (53:2–9), observers wrote him off as useless.

53:10–12. The servant has died, so his vindication must occur beyond the span of earthly life. But the exact nature of it is not described.

These verses emphasize the servant's willingness to accept the suffering given to him. Verse 53:10 can be rendered "When *he made himself* an offering for sin." God vindicates the servant "because *he poured out himself* to death" and because, as the next words can be translated, *"he let himself* be numbered with the transgressors" (53:12; italics mine). The servant's absolute obedience to God is essential to his mission of undoing the effects of people's disobedience to the Creator.

The servant's suffering not only releases the guilty from punishment. It also leads the guilty to repentance; it changes hearts and makes us whole (53:5). How can this be? Isaiah has not explained. His words leave many questions unanswered. When Jesus arrives, the mysterious image of the servant will come into focus. Even so, God's life-giving action through Jesus' humiliation and suffering will remain forever a mystery.

Questions for Application

40 minutes
Choose questions according to your interest and time.

---

1 Who is despised and rejected today? What does this week's reading suggest about those whom people consider "of no account"?

---

2 In what ways do sickness and infirmity cut people off from social life today? What can be done to overcome this exclusion? How could you reach out to someone who is isolated by sickness or misfortune?

---

3 When have you witnessed God acting through the suffering caused by sickness or injustice? How has this affected your thinking about God?

---

4 The servant seems to lack political, economic, and military power. What kind of power does he have? Who in the world today exercises the servant's kind of power?

5 When have you had the experience of being close to someone else in their suffering? Have you ever suffered along with someone who is suffering the consequences of their own poor choices? How did this experience affect you? How might this week's reading from Isaiah enter into your reflections?

6 How might this week's reading contribute to your mental picture of Jesus? How might this affect how you relate to him?

When the discussion wanders away from the Bible, you may need to get the group back on track by saying, "What we're discussing is interesting, but we've left our topic."

How to Lead Small Group Bible Studies

Approach to Prayer

15 minutes
Use this approach—or create your own!

- Slowly and meditatively pray Psalm 22 aloud (different members of the group can take turns reading). End with a Glory to the Father. You may wish to set up a crucifix in the place where you pray.

A Living Tradition

Be Like Jesus, the Servant of All

This section is a supplement for individual reading.

Isaiah's poems about the servant of the Lord cast an interpretive light on Jesus' crucifixion. The Servant Songs help us perceive the saving dimension of Jesus' death—the dimension that was hidden from most of those who watched him expire on the cross. Isaiah's words not only deepen our understanding of the meaning of Jesus' death; they also illuminate the example of humble service that Jesus has given us to follow. It is this latter aspect of the poem—the servant as a model for imitation—that is featured in its first known Christian use outside the New Testament.

The writer was a man named Clement who, according to early Church tradition, was a bishop of Rome in the last decade of the first century. During this period, some Christians in Corinth drove the leaders of their community from office and tried to replace them. Clement sent the community in Corinth a long letter urging the Christians there to respect the order of the Church and be reconciled with one another. He insisted that humility was crucial for a restoration of unity, and he offered the Suffering Servant Song as a sketch of the humility of Jesus, which Jesus' followers are called to make their own. Apparently Clement felt that the Suffering Servant Song spoke for itself, for he quoted it at length, adding only these few words of commentary:

Christ belongs to those whose attitude is humble, not to those who lift themselves up and set themselves over his flock. Even though he is the scepter of the divine magnificence, the Lord Jesus Christ did not come with boasting, false pretensions, and arrogance. Despite his power, he was humble in his thinking, as the Holy Spirit spoke of him, saying, "Who has believed . . . " [here Clement quotes Isaiah 53 in its entirety]. My dear friends, you see what model has been given to us! If the *Lord* was so humble, what shall *we* do, now that we have come under the yoke of his grace?

From *1 Clement 16*

Week 6

My Love Shall Not Depart

Questions to Begin

15 minutes
Use a question or two to get warmed up for the reading.

1. Do you like to camp? If not, what do you like to do on vacation?

2. Describe a situation in which you were reconciled with someone after a breach in the relationship.

3. Who in your experience has been an example of faithfulness?

Opening the Bible

5 minutes
Read the passage aloud. Let individuals take turns reading. (Suggestion: first speaker—54:1–3; second speaker—54:7–10; third speaker—54:11–14; fourth speaker—55:6–7; fifth speaker—55:8–11.)

The Reading: Isaiah 54:1–14; 55:6–11

Good News for the Abandoned Wife

1 Sing, O barren one who did not bear;
burst into song and shout,
you who have not been in labor!
For the children of the desolate woman will be more
than the children of her that is married, says the LORD.
2 Enlarge the site of your tent,
and let the curtains of your habitations be stretched out;
do not hold back; lengthen your cords
and strengthen your stakes.
3 For you will spread out to the right and to the left,
and your descendants will possess the nations
and will settle the desolate towns. . . .

7 For a brief moment I abandoned you,
but with great compassion I will gather you.
8 In overflowing wrath for a moment
I hid my face from you,
but with everlasting love I will have compassion on you,
says the LORD, your Redeemer. . . .

10 For the mountains may depart
and the hills be removed,
but my steadfast love shall not depart from you,
and my covenant of peace shall not be removed,
says the LORD, who has compassion on you.

The Returning Husband Speaks

11 O afflicted one, storm-tossed, and not comforted,
I am about to set your stones in antimony,
and lay your foundations with sapphires.
12 I will make your pinnacles of rubies,
your gates of jewels,
and all your wall of precious stones.

[13] All your children shall be taught by the Lord,
and great shall be the prosperity of your children.
[14] In righteousness you shall be established;
you shall be far from oppression, for you shall not fear;
and from terror, for it shall not come near you. . . .

God's Promises Will Not Fail

[55:6] Seek the LORD while he may be found,
call upon him while he is near;
[7] let the wicked forsake their way,
and the unrighteous their thoughts;
let them return to the Lord, that he may have mercy on them,
and to our God, for he will abundantly pardon.
[8] For my thoughts are not your thoughts,
nor are your ways my ways, says the LORD.
[9] For as the heavens are higher than the earth,
so are my ways higher than your ways
and my thoughts than your thoughts.

[10] For as the rain and the snow come down from heaven,
and do not return there until they have watered the earth,
making it bring forth and sprout,
giving seed to the sower and bread to the eater,
[11] so shall my word be that goes out from my mouth;
it shall not return to me empty,
but it shall accomplish that which I purpose,
and succeed in the thing for which I sent it.

Questions for Careful Reading

10 minutes
Choose questions according to your interest and time.

1 What is the "moment" in 54:7? How "brief" was it? (You might wish to refer to page 8.)

2 How would you restate the promises to Jerusalem (54:1–14) in nonpoetic terms?

3 What is the similarity between 54:11 and 40:1? How might the two passages shed light on each other's meaning?

4 In 54:11, what is "antimony"? (Consult a dictionary if necessary.)

5 What is the "word" referred to in 55:11?

6 What purpose is served by placing 55:6–11 virtually at the end of Second Isaiah's prophecies?

A Guide to the Reading

If participants have not read this section already, read it aloud. Otherwise go on to "Questions for Application."

54:1–3. The suffering servant has cleared the way for people to be reconciled with God. Chapter 54 celebrates the reconciliation with marriage imagery. The Lord is reunited with Lady Jerusalem with a renewal of marriage vows (54:7–8) and a promise of children (54:1–3). Verse 1 contrasts depopulated but about-to-be-restored Jerusalem with prosperous but about-to-be-defeated Babylon. (That the Lord asks Lady Jerusalem to perform the tent-enlarging tasks is apt: among ancient Near Easterners, putting up tents was women's work.)

The prophecy alludes to the past in order to strengthen the people's faith. God's promise that "the children of the desolate woman will be more than the children of her that is married" recalls the rejoicing of Hannah: "The barren has borne seven, but she who has many children is forlorn" (1 Samuel 2:5). As Paul Hanson remarks, "The God who was able to bless the barren matriarch of old surely is able to do so again." The promise that "your descendants will possess the nations" (54:3) echoes God's promise of offspring to Abraham (Genesis 22:17). Surely the God who fulfilled that promise will fulfill his new promise of restoration to the exiles and to those who remain in Judea.

54:7–10. God acknowledges that "for a brief moment" he abandoned his people. That is to say, he withdrew his protection from them and let their enemies defeat them. The period of defeat and exile may seem short to God, but it must have seemed endless to the people who were stuck in the generation-long period of suffering. But then, who abandoned whom? Only when the people of Jerusalem refused to listen to prophetic appeals to return to the path of justice did God let the forces of disintegration overwhelm them.

The restored marriage between God and his people will be built on his "everlasting love." The Hebrew word is the same one Isaiah used for "constancy" at the beginning, when he asked God, "Why bother speaking to people who lack constancy?" (see 40:6). God now gives his answer: since the people lack the faithfulness needed to keep the marriage going, God will undergird the relationship with his own faithful love.

A caution is in order with regard to this marriage imagery. In the Bible, when marriage imagery is used for God's relationship with his people, God is represented by the husband, Israel by the wife (Hosea 1–2). Thus in this imagery the man is always in the right while the woman is often guilty of unfaithfulness. The danger is that this imagery may foster an unbalanced view of marriage. Despite this danger, however, marriage imagery is irreplaceable, for what image could better express the intimacy and intensity, the longing and self-giving—as well as the frustration and pain—of God's relationship with his human creatures?

54:11–14. Jerusalem will need protective walls if she is to enjoy prosperity and peace. The picture of a city set with precious stones may draw on ancient Near Eastern myths of paradise (compare Ezekiel 28:13–14). Thus the restored Jerusalem will be paradise regained. The image of a perfect city is taken up again in the Bible's final prophecy of God's dwelling with the human race (Revelation 21:19–21). The urban imagery suggests that God's plan for our eternity is emphatically social.

But a happy Jerusalem will need more than stone walls. Verses 54:13–14 make it clear that the people's welfare will depend on their commitment to God's instructions for their lives and their "righteousness"—that is, justice—in their dealings with one another.

55:6–11. The prophet concludes with a last attempt to pry the Israelites out of their discouragement. When it comes to leaving Babylon for Jerusalem, there may be various reasons why the exiles' "thoughts" are different from God's "thoughts" (55:8). Undoubtedly some of them have become comfortable in Babylon and are reluctant to give up the satisfactions of their settled life in exchange for a dimly remembered homeland. Others probably consider Isaiah's vision an impossible utopia. God's declaration of his creative power is designed to meet both objections.

God declares that his word will "succeed" (55:11). This connects with the earlier declaration that the purpose of the Lord will "prosper" through the servant (53:10), for the same Hebrew verb is used in both instances. Ultimately Jesus, who is both God's incarnate Word and his suffering servant, will bring to success all of God's plans for the human race.

Questions for Application

40 minutes
Choose questions according to your interest and time.

---

1 What attitudes and actions are important for reconciliation between individual persons? What can this human experience teach us about reconciliation with God?

---

2 Do God's promises of eternal life seem too good to be true? Do they seem too distant to make much difference in how you live today? What might this reading offer to your reflections on this subject?

---

3 In what situations in your life might God's words in 54:10 have particular meaning for you?

---

4 How might God's faithfulness to his word be an example for you to imitate in your relationships with other people?

5 God addresses himself to exiles who are "afflicted" (54:11)—poor, wretched, overwhelmed by want. As biblical scholar Klaus Baltzer remarks, they are "those who are denied justice, who possess no influence or status, who are at the mercy of opponents with unlimited power." God intends to reverse their situation. As a servant of God's kingdom, how are you called to cooperate with him in his justice-bringing activity in the world?

6 What experiences in your life come to mind when you read 55:8–9?

The Bible is not just a book to be read and studied. It contains God's word, which should be the object of our prayerful meditation. As a source of inspiration and spiritual nourishment, the Bible ought to be a constant companion.

National Conference of Catholic Bishops, *Sharing the Light of Faith*

Approach to Prayer

15 minutes
Use this approach—or create your own!

- Pray a Glory to the Father. Take turns reading aloud these mini-hymns celebrating God's love for his people: Isaiah 51:11–16; 52:7–10; 55:1–3; 55:12–13. Allow time for any who wish to express individual prayers. Close with an Our Father.

Saints in the Making

Waiting for God's Word to Be Fulfilled

This section is a supplement for individual reading.

One day in 1839, in Saint-Servan in Brittany, France, an elderly woman named Anne Haneau came to the apartment of Jeanne Jugan and Francoise Aubert looking for help. Blind, sick, and without any means of support, Haneau was in desperate need. The pair took her in, and Jugan gave up her bed to the older woman. Not long after, Jugan and Aubert took in another elderly woman, Isabelle Coeuru. Jugan, who was forty-seven, was a prayerful woman with experience in caring for sick and elderly people. She sensed that Christ was giving her an invitation to serve by sending Haneau and Coeuru to her home. Soon the apartment Jugan shared with Aubert was home to several more indigent women. Within a year, they moved to larger quarters to accommodate their guests, and other women began to give them assistance. These were the beginnings of a religious congregation called the Little Sisters of the Poor.

The local bishop asked a priest in Saint-Servan named LePailleur to provide Jugan and her associates with guidance. Father LePailleur soon began to assert that the association had been *his* idea. An "unfortunate psychopath," as one later writer calls him, LePailleur removed Jugan from leadership of the association and replaced her with a more compliant woman.

Fearing that conflict with LePailleur would damage the association and its service to the elderly, Jugan silently accepted interior exile in her own association—for *twenty-seven years*! She trusted that the one who had called her to the work was the God who declared to Isaiah, "my word . . . shall not return to me empty, but it shall accomplish that which I purpose, and succeed in the thing for which I sent it" (55:11).

Only after Jugan's death did Church authorities uncover LePailleur's manipulation and free the association from his grip. But Jugan's years in obscurity were not wasted. Her banishment from leadership put her in close contact with the younger women who were being trained for membership in the association. This gave her the opportunity to share with them her trust in God and love for the poor. Her dismissal from leadership of the association had put her in the best position to shape its future.

What Happened after That?

The prophet of Isaiah 40 through 55 made sweeping promises in God's name. How did they pan out?

Within a decade or so of Isaiah's prophesying, a string of lightning victories brought the Persian ruler Cyrus to power over the entire Near East. He toppled the Babylonian empire in 538 B.C. Soon after—some fifty years after the Babylonians had sacked Jerusalem—Cyrus instituted a policy that allowed Israelite exiles and their descendants to return home. The fulfillment of Isaiah's prophecies had gotten off to a dramatic start.

From that point on, however, the course of events increasingly diverged from the glorious picture that Isaiah had projected. Some Jews in Babylon trickled homeward to Judea, but their road was not paved with miracles (Ezra 1–2; 8; compare Isaiah 41:17–20; 42:15–16; 55:12–13). On their return, they became mired in disagreements with Jews who had remained in the land (Ezra 4:1–4). The community was beset with economic difficulties and hostile neighbors (Ezra 4; Nehemiah 4; Haggai 1). Rather than suddenly morphing into a prosperous metropolis ringed by splendid fortifications, Jerusalem remained in ruins for decades and was only slowly and laboriously rebuilt and repopulated (Nehemiah 1–7; 11; compare Isaiah 54:11–17).

Determined not to repeat past mistakes, the restored community strove to avoid the injustices that had earlier led to disintegration and defeat (Nehemiah 8–9). But their follow-through fell short of their intentions (Nehemiah 5; compare Isaiah 54:13–14). And their efforts at faithfulness to God's law were marred by exclusivity—a narrow focus on ethnic purity and on those aspects of the Mosaic law that marked Jews as distinct from others (Ezra 4:3; 9–10; Nehemiah 13; compare Isaiah 49:6).

Eventually the Persian empire also fell (333 B.C.), and the Jews came under the domination of a Greek-speaking regime based in Antioch (in present-day Turkey). Around 165 B.C., this regime launched an effort to suppress Jewish religion and culture. Some Jews faced the persecution with loyalty to their God-given traditions (2 Maccabees 6–7). Others promoted compromise with the polytheistic Greek culture (1 Maccabees 1:11–15). The scene of external persecution and internal division hardly reflected the secure and righteous city that Isaiah had foreseen.

In reaction to the persecution, some Jews tried to finally regain national independence, lost four centuries earlier. Led by a family called the Maccabees, they succeeded in ejecting the Greek-speaking occupiers (1 Maccabees 2–16) and set up a kind of religious dictatorship. Their regime, called the Hasmonean dynasty, created sharp divisions within the Jewish community and collapsed in less than a century. In 63 B.C., the Jewish homeland fell under the control of an empire larger and more powerful than that of Babylon, Persia, or Syria: the empire of Rome.

Thus, five centuries after Isaiah's prophesying, his vision of a restored Israelite society was largely unrealized. Yet the prophet's final words had expressed God's guarantee that the prophetic announcement would bear fruit (55:6–13), and many Jews earnestly looked forward to its fulfillment—although they had various notions regarding what the fulfillment would look like and how they were supposed to cooperate with its coming.

Into this situation entered Jesus of Nazareth.

Significantly, all four Gospel writers connect Jesus' ministry with the promises of Isaiah 40–55. The evangelists make the connection by opening their accounts of Jesus' ministry with a quotation from the beginning of Second Isaiah's prophecies. They apply Isaiah 40:3 ("A voice cries out: 'In the wilderness prepare the way of the Lord'") to the man who prepared the way for Jesus: John the Baptist (Matthew 3:3; Mark 1:1–4; Luke 3:4–6; John 1:23). Preaching by the Jordan River in the barren region east of Jerusalem, John was literally a voice crying out in the wilderness. Isaiah's words applied to him in a strikingly direct fashion: Isaiah had announced that the Lord was coming to his people ("See, the Lord God comes"—40:10); John announced that the Lord was indeed coming, in the flesh. By their reference to Isaiah 40:3, the evangelists implied that the expectations aroused by Isaiah would receive fulfillment through Jesus. In Jesus, God would reveal his "glory" (40:5)—he would intervene compassionately and decisively in human affairs.

After his death and resurrection, Jesus' followers discovered numerous ways that Isaiah 40–55 shed light on his identity and the meaning of his ministry. Isaiah predicted God's restoration of Israel and the impact that restoration would have on the whole world (45:22–23; 49:6; 52:15). These predictions provided the early Christians with images that expressed their sense of calling to bring the good news about Jesus to people beyond the boundaries of Judaism (this theme was especially important to St. Paul: Romans 10:15–16; 15:21; Philippians 2:10).

The prophecies we have explored in Isaiah found striking fulfillment in Jesus' life, death, and resurrection:

- Isaiah foretold that the Lord was coming to end his people's exile. By reconciling human beings with God through his death and resurrection, Jesus makes possible our return from the most profound exile of all—the exile of sin, of alienation from God and one another.
- Isaiah proclaimed God's forgiveness to people who had hardly begun to perceive the seriousness of their sins. Jesus' ministry and, above all, his reconciling death embodied God's reaching out to us while we are yet sinners, even before we recognize our need for his grace (Romans 5:6–11).
- In his concern for the uprooted Israelites, God showed a preferential love for the needy. This love reached perfect expression in Jesus, who extends mercy to every man and woman suffering the poverty of sin and longing for the power to love.
- Isaiah sketched a portrait of a suffering servant of God. In his crucifixion, Jesus gave himself to God's purposes so completely that he suffered the effects of our sins in order to remove them.

Although Jesus fulfilled the expectations of God's action aroused by Isaiah, God did not then stamp Isaiah 40–55 "paid in full" and file it away as a record of completed dealings with the human race. Isaiah's words, fulfilled by Jesus, are now directed toward us, Jesus' followers. God has entrusted to us the message of his grace, the message of the reconciliation that Jesus has accomplished, so that we might bring it to the people around us. We convey the message not only by speaking it but also by embodying it, especially by demonstrating God's love for all who are poor, needy, and oppressed. Jesus invites us to take on the role of the suffering servant in imitation of him: to embrace a life of humble obedience to God, to unite ourselves with him in self-giving for others, to live in solidarity with those who suffer.

In a further way, also, Isaiah's prophecies are not merely a thing of the past. Jesus' full realization of Isaiah's promises lies in the future. Indeed, it lies beyond all future time in a new creation. Jesus and his early followers used Isaiah's images of a marriage between God and his people and of God's people gathered securely in a peaceful city (chapter 54) to describe the ultimate fulfillment of God's intentions for the human race (Matthew 22:1–14; Revelation 19:9; 21–22).

And so we return to the point where we began, to discouragement. No simple formula can banish our experiences of darkness, for no formula can uproot the causes of grief and sorrow in earthly life. But in the coming of Christ, the ultimate displacement of our sorrow has begun. Jesus declared, "Blessed are those who mourn, for they will be comforted" (Matthew 5:4). God's kingdom of reconciliation and peace has already become present among us. This kingdom gives us the hope of an eternity in which death and sorrow will be swallowed up in life and joy.

The Spirit of God directs our attention toward this kingdom already present. He urges us to cooperate with the coming of this kingdom in our world. This is good therapy for our discouragement, for it is in serving others that we find distraction from our own sorrows and experience most powerfully God's kingdom already mysteriously present among us. The Spirit invites us to turn our eyes toward the eternal goal that God has in mind for us (Romans 8:18–39)—a goal beautifully suggested by the poetry of Isaiah.

Suggestions for Bible Discussion Groups

Like a camping trip, a Bible discussion group works best if you agree on where you're going and how you intend to get there. Many groups use their first meeting to talk over such questions and reach a consensus. Here is a checklist of issues, with bits of advice from people who have experience in Bible discussions. (A planning discussion will go more smoothly if the leaders have thought through the following issues beforehand.)

Agree on your purpose. Are you getting together to gain wisdom and direction for your lives? to finally get acquainted with the Bible? to support one another in following Christ? to encourage those who are exploring—or reexploring—the Church? for other reasons?

Agree on attitudes. For example: "We're all beginners here." "We're here to help each other understand and respond to God's word." "We're not here to offer counseling or direction to each other." "We want to read Scripture prayerfully." What do *you* wish to emphasize? Make it explicit!

Agree on ground rules. Barbara J. Fleischer, in her useful book *Facilitating for Growth,* recommends that a group clearly state its approach to the following:

- *Preparation.* Do we agree to read the material and prepare the answers to the questions before each meeting?
- *Attendance.* What kind of priority will we give to our meetings?
- *Self-revelation.* Are we willing to help the others in the group gradually get to know us—our weaknesses as well as our strengths, our needs as well as our gifts?
- *Listening.* Will we commit ourselves to listening to each other?
- *Confidentiality.* Will we keep everything that is shared *with* the group *in* the group?
- *Discretion.* Will we refrain from sharing about the faults and sins of people outside the group?
- *Encouragement and support.* Will we give as well as receive?
- *Participation.* Will we give each person time and opportunity to make a contribution?

You could probably take a pen and draw a circle around *listening* and *confidentiality.* Those two points are especially important.

The following items could be added to Fleischer's list:

- *Relationship with parish.* Is our group part of the adult faith-formation program? independent but operating with the express approval of the pastor? not a parish-based group?
- *New members.* Will we let new members join us once we have begun the six weeks of discussions?

Agree on housekeeping.

- *When will we meet?*
- *How often will we meet?* Meeting weekly or every other week is best if you can manage it. William Riley remarks, "Meetings once a month are too distant from each other for the threads of the last session not to be lost" *(The Bible Study Group: An Owner's Manual).*
- *How long will meetings run?*
- *Where will we meet?*
- *Is any setup needed?* Christine Dodd writes that "the problem with meeting in a place like a church hall is that it can be very soul-destroying" given the cold, impersonal feel of many church facilities. If you have to meet in a church facility, Dodd recommends doing something to make the area homey *(Making Scripture Work).*
- *Who will host the meetings?* Leaders and hosts are not necessarily the same people.
- *Will we have refreshments?* Who will provide them?
- *What about child care?* Most experienced leaders of Bible discussion groups discourage bringing infants or other children to adult Bible discussions.

Agree on leadership. You need someone to facilitate—to keep the discussion on track, to see that everyone has a chance to speak, to help the group stay on schedule. Rena Duff, editor of the newsletter *Sharing God's Word Today,* recommends having two or three people take turns leading the discussions.

It's okay if the leader is not an expert on the Bible. You have this booklet, and if questions come up that no one can answer, you can delegate a participant to do a little research between meetings. It's important for the leader to set an example of listening, to draw out the quieter members (and occasionally restrain the more vocal ones), to move the group on when it gets stuck, to remind the members of their agreements, and to summarize what the group is accomplishing.

Bible discussion is an opportunity to experience the fulfillment of Jesus' promise "Where two or three are gathered in my name, I am there among them" (Matthew 18:20). Put your discussion group in Jesus' hands. Pray for the guidance of the Spirit. And have a great time exploring God's word together!

Suggestions for Individuals

You can use this booklet just as well for individual study as for group discussion. While discussing the Bible with other people can be a rich experience, there are advantages to reading on your own. For example:

- You can focus on the points that interest you most.
- You can go at your own pace.
- You can be completely relaxed and unashamedly honest in your answers to all the questions, since you don't have to share them with anyone!

My suggestions for using this booklet on your own are these:

- Don't skip "Questions to Begin." The questions can help you as an individual reader warm up to the topic of the reading.
- Take your time on "Questions for Careful Reading" and "Questions for Application." While a group will probably not have enough time to work on all the questions, you can allow yourself the time to consider all of them if you are using the booklet by yourself.
- After reading the "Guide to the Reading," go back and reread the Scripture text before answering the questions for application.
- Take the time to look up all the parenthetical Scripture references.
- Since you control the pace, give yourself plenty of opportunities to reflect on the meaning of Isaiah 40–55 for you. Let your reading be an opportunity for these words to become God's words to you.

Resources

Bibles

The following editions of the Bible contain the full set of biblical books recognized by the Catholic Church, along with a great deal of useful explanatory material:

- The Catholic Study Bible (Oxford University Press), which uses the text of the New American Bible
- The Catholic Bible: Personal Study Edition (Oxford University Press), which also uses the text of the New American Bible
- The New Jerusalem Bible, the regular (not the reader's) edition (Doubleday)

Books

- Walter Brueggemann, *Isaiah,* Westminster Bible Companion (Louisville, Ky.: Westminster John Knox Press, 1998).
- John J. Collins, "Isaiah," in *The Collegeville Bible Commentary: Based on the New American Bible with Revised New Testament,* ed. Dianne Bergant and Robert J. Karris (Collegeville, Minn.: Liturgical Press, 1989), 411–52.
- Paul D. Hanson, *Isaiah 40–66,* Interpretation, A Bible Commentary for Teaching and Preaching (Louisville, Ky.: John Knox Press, 1995).
- Claus Westermann, *Isaiah 40–66: A Commentary,* The Old Testament Library (Philadelphia: Westminster Press, 1969).

How has Scripture had an impact on your life? Was this booklet helpful to you in your study of the Bible? Please send comments, suggestions, and personal experiences to Kevin Perrotta, c/o Trade Editorial Department, Loyola Press, 3441 N. Ashland Ave., Chicago, IL 60657.

Notes

Notes